SALVADOR
DALI

SALVADOR

DALI

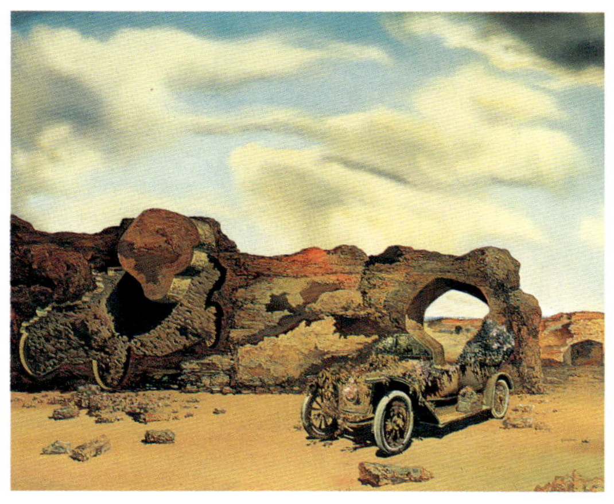

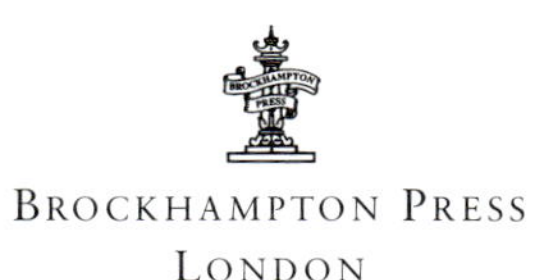

BROCKHAMPTON PRESS
LONDON

TITLE PAGE

Paranoiac - Critical Solitude. 1935

The image is another example of the bizarre juxtaposition of images by the Surrealists. Dali seems to comment on the impermanence of material acquisition with the decaying car. This image anticipates his controversial *Rainy Taxi* installation at the 1938 International Surrealist Exhibition in Paris.

THE LIFE AND WORK of Salvador Dali (1904 - 1989) generates extreme reactions. His story is underpinned by a series of paradoxes; born into a liberal, republican, affluent Spanish family, he came to be both monarchist and Catholic in later life; his art symbolised the Surrealist avant-garde of the 1930s, but its' technique was founded on the discredited academic principles of the nineteenth century; he generated immense wealth from his work and idiosyncratic public profile, yet professed to despise late industrial capitalist society, and those members of it who fawned on him.

Dali began his training at the local drawing school at Figueras, under the academic painter Juan Nunez, learning academic compositional techniques and absorbing the works of Old Masters who were to fascinate him:

Vermeer, Velazquez and Millet. Five years at the School of Fine Arts in Madrid were valuable only in terms of his exposure to the techniques of Parisian modernism, and the contacts he made.

Repeated insubordination led to Dali's expulsion from Madrid in 1926. After successful exhibitions in Barcelona and collaboration with Bunuel over the film *Un Chien Andalou*, Dali's first Parisian exhibition in 1929 cemented his arrival at the forefront of the Surrealist avant-garde.

The work from 1929-c.1932 is predominantly erotic, focusing on common sexual neuroses. Recurring themes and icons become clear in this period: insects, decay, guilt, mutilation, the grotesque. Steadily, Dali developed his own approach to painting, dubbed the 'paranoiac-critical' method. This involved the inducement of a state of delirium so that Dali could reproduce the images of a madman without any diminution of his critical faculties. The method saw Dali move towards fantastic and dream-like images, allowing him to address broader concerns such as the Spanish Civil War.

With the capitulation of France in 1940, the painter fled to New York. He continued to be interested in new developments, however, both in art and science, praising the work of the abstract expressionists and fascinated by newly developed atomic power. Moreover, his imagery mirrors an increasingly fervent affiliation with the Catholic Church.

After the death of his wife Gala in 1982, Dali spent his declining years in isolation. He died as a result of a fourth heart attack in January 1989, leaving behind a series of impenetrable myths and works that, whatever one's opinion of them, stand as icons of the early twentieth century.

THE BURNING GIRAFFE, 1936-7. *right*

Dali seems to portray his ideas of the 'primitive' in this painting, an issue of great interest for Surrealists. The burning giraffe makes reference to the idea of ritual sacrifice, and also has Freudian connotations of impotence and sexual failure. The dancing human ciphers in the foreground stress the importance of the loss of self-consciousness in the dance and in creative activity in general.

COMPOSITION: EVOCATION OF LENIN, 1931. *overleaf*

The origin of this image derives from one of the painter's childhood experiences, where he was punished by being locked up in a darkened cellar. Lenin was an icon of Dali's output in the early thirties, and here he wittily appears as a mystic visionary. Insects, seen crawling over the music stand, are another favourite Dalinean leitmotif, denoting decay and one of the painter's personal symbols of eroticism.

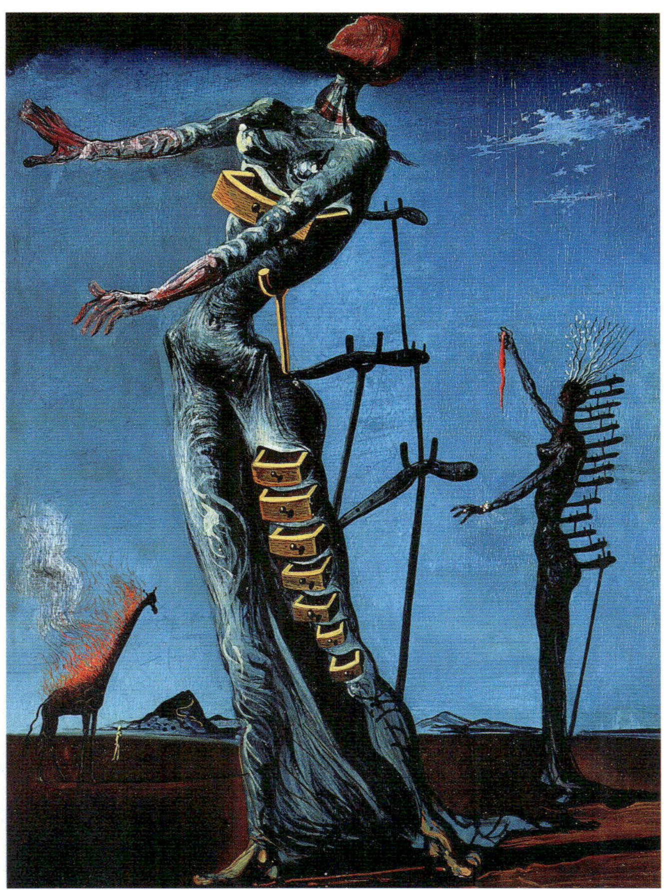

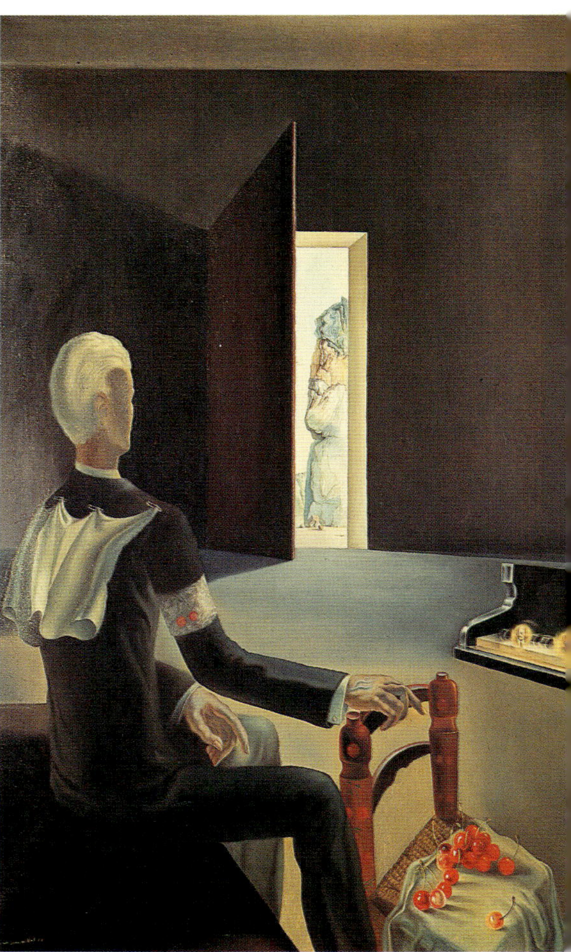

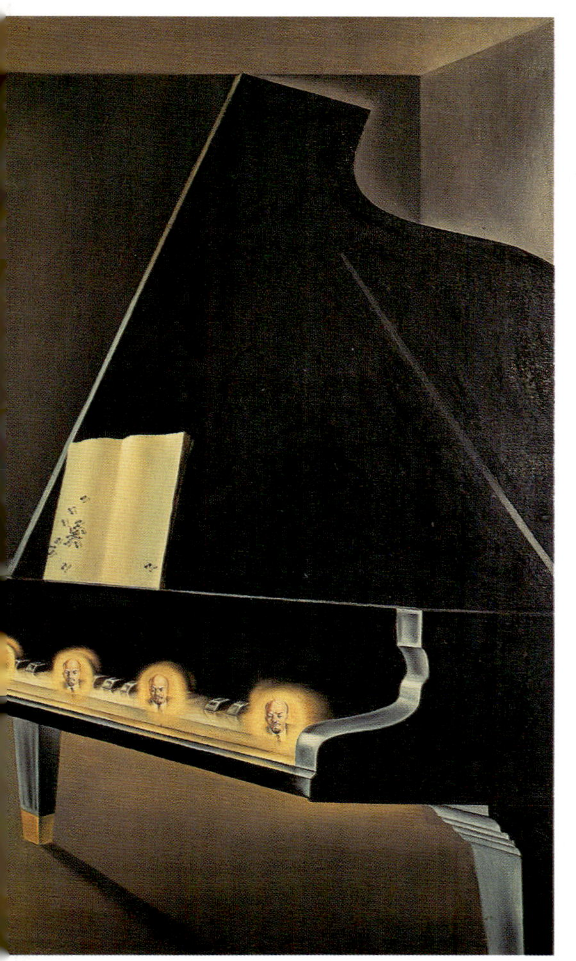

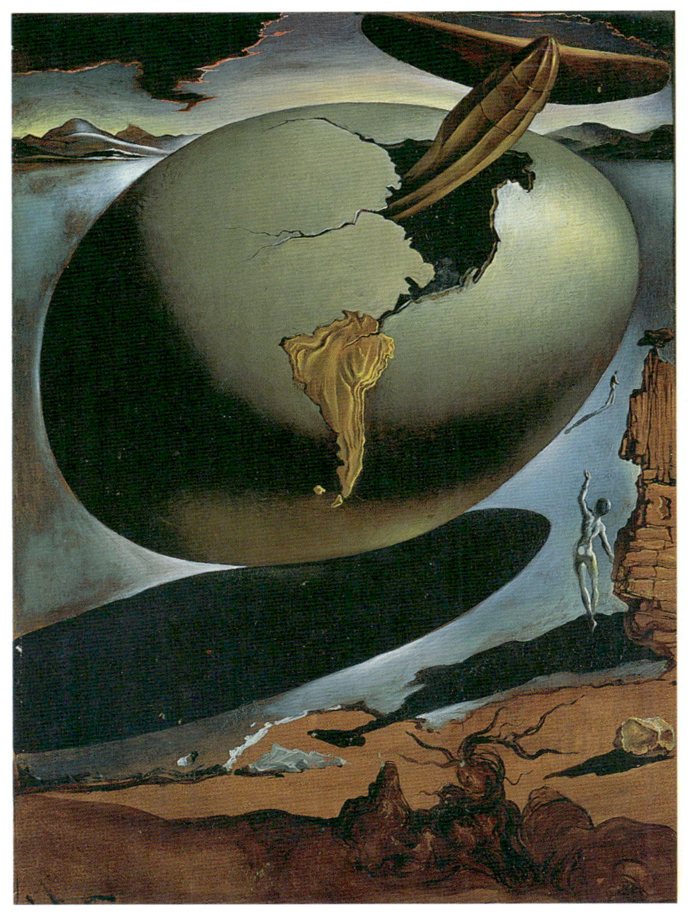

Allegory on an American Christmas, 1934. *left*
This work taps into fears in thirties Europe, that American capitalist ideas threatened indigenous cultures and customs. A crashed aircraft has left a giant American-shaped crater in an egg-shaped globe, which is menacingly balanced above a solitary figure beneath.

Suburb of the Paranoiac - Critical Town; Afternoon on the Outskirts of European History, 1936. *overleaf*
Here Dali employs the classic Surrealist technique of juxtaposing contradictory images on one canvas. He comments indirectly on the historical influences which have engaged his attention; some Raphaelesque architecture in the left hand corner, the Edwardian oddities and fashion items in the foreground, and the haunting street architecture of the Italian painter Giorgio de Chirico at right.

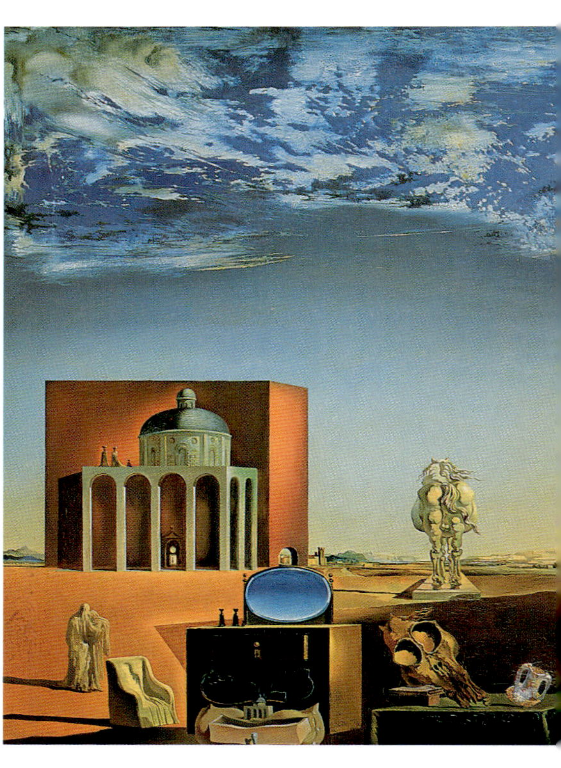

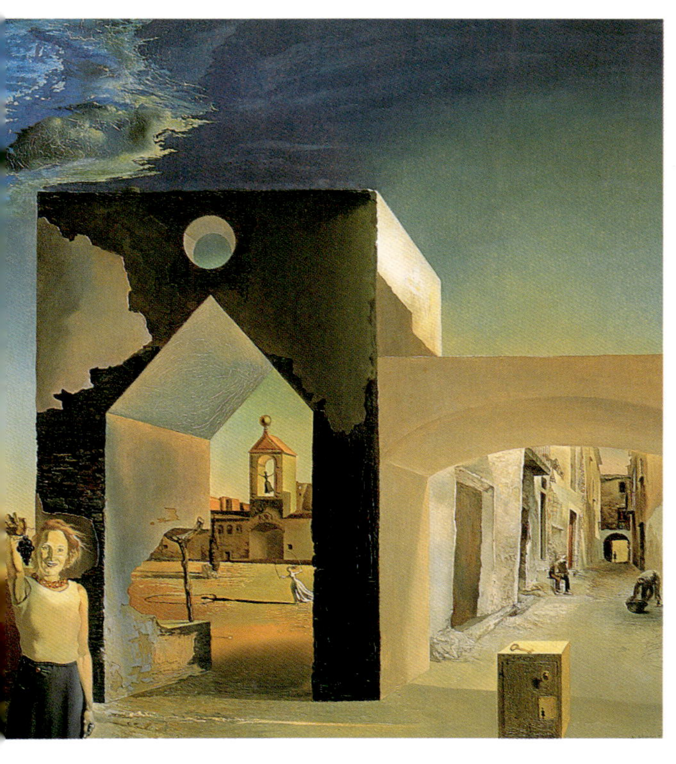

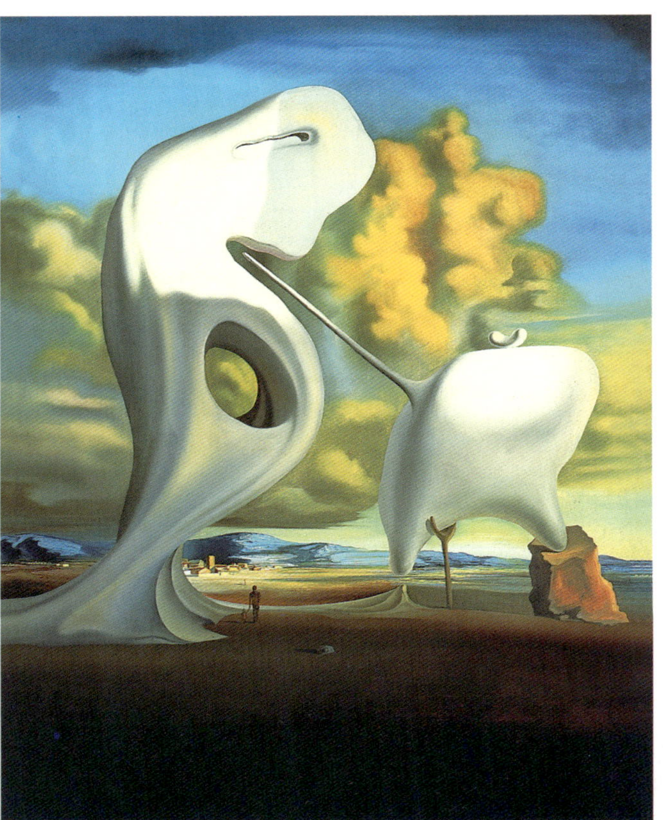

The Architectonic Angelus of Millet, 1933. *left*
The painter was obsessed by Millet's 1859 work, *Angelus*. The two peasants in Millet's painting have been transformed into vast rock-like white shapes, and their biomorphic, atavistic shapes suggest an attempt by Dali to ground his practice in the earliest roots of the visual tradition.

Image Mediumnique - Paranoique, 1935. *overleaf*
Dali's ability to create a vast pictorial space is apparent here. The inspiration for this picture came from a visit to the Costa Brava, and typical features include the menacing sky and the self-absorbed isolation of the figures. The motif of the two peasants labouring at the bottom right of the painting may come from the work of the Dutch nineteenth century realists, The Hague School.

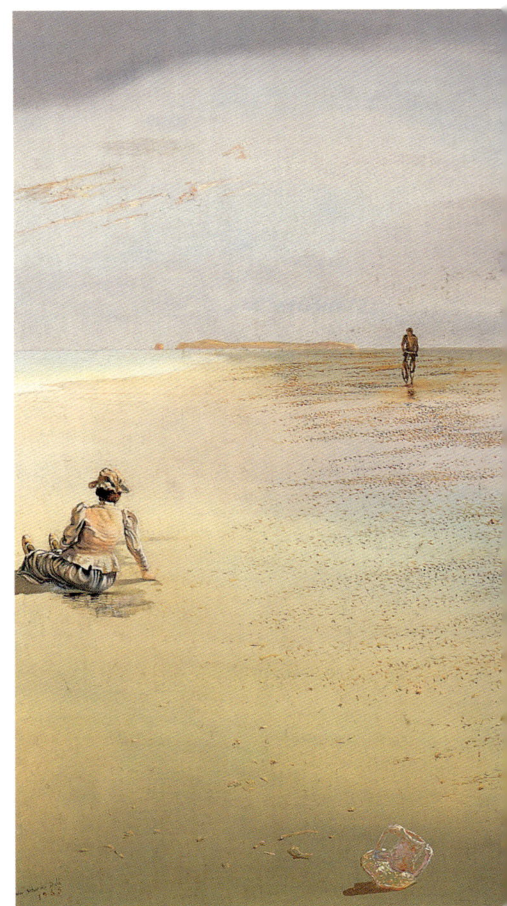

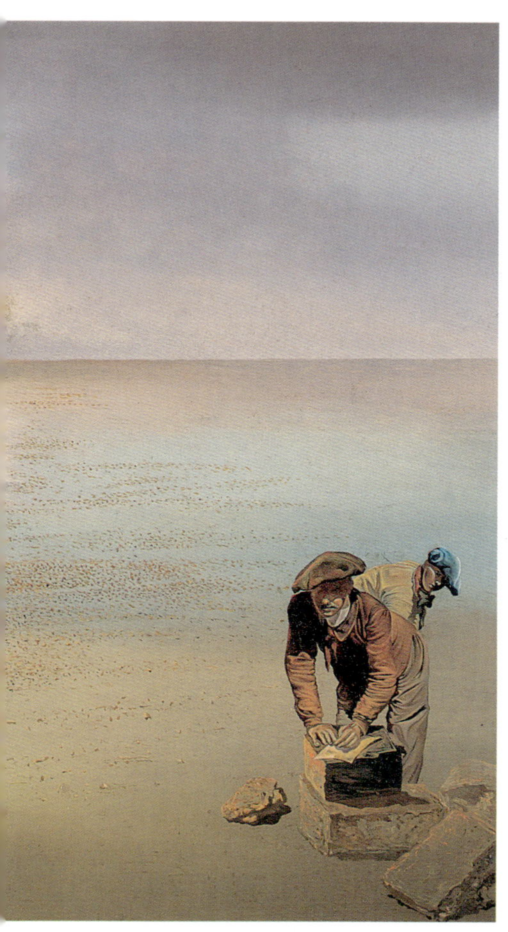

THE HAIR (LA CHEVELURE), 1931. *right*

Dali plays on the naturalistic associations of hair, with the patterns echoing those of tree-rings and geological formations. The seaside image visible may link back to the painter's fascination with lewd Edwardian postcards- particularly in the garish screen at the centre of the painting, and the couple at the water's edge.

THE ENIGMA OF DESIRE: MY MOTHER, MY MOTHER, MY MOTHER, 1929. *overleaf*

One of the early erotic works. Dali makes clear reference to the Oedipus myth, and the lion's head is another sexual symbol which he frequently employs. His painterly technique leaves no trace of the brushwork, echoing the high standard of finish practised by nineteenth century neo-classical 'Pompier' artists.

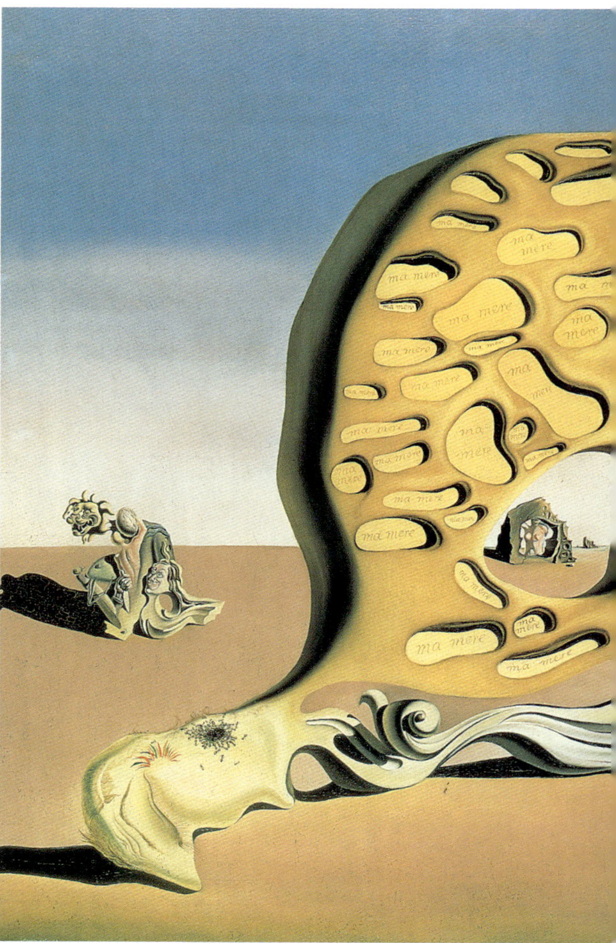
ma mère
ma mère
ma mère
ma mère
ma mère
ma mère
ma mère
ma mère
ma mère
ma mère
ma mère
ma mère
ma mère
ma mère
ma mère
ma mère
ma mère
ma mère
ma mère

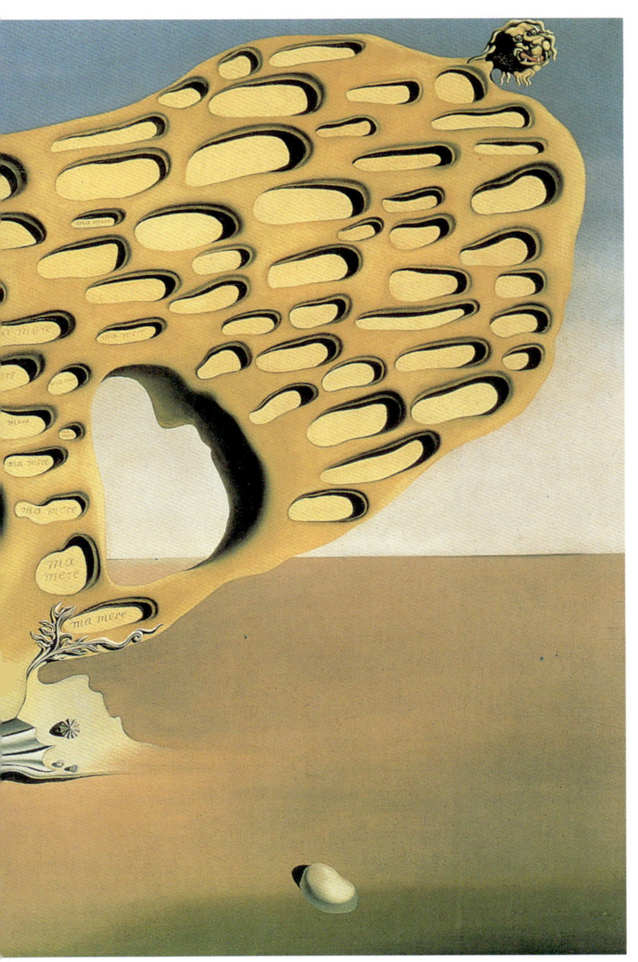
ma mere
ma mere
ma mere
ma mere
ma
mere
ma mere

LAURENCE OLIVIER IN THE ROLE OF RICHARD III, 1955. *right* This portrait attempts to fuse the Renaissance with the modern. The detail on the sword, belt and medal evokes the profile portraiture of Mantegna and Piero, whilst the double image makes reference to Cubist developments. At the same time the double image is a literary reference to the treacherous nature of the Shakespearean King.

SWANS, REFLECTING ELEPHANTS, 1937. *overleaf* A good example of a mature 'paranoiac-critical' image. Dali has engaged in a game of shape association and has produced an unlikely juxtaposition. The dense layering of images in this canvas contrasts abundant growth with putrefaction: the clouds, shaped like human forms, hold the key to the associative source of the painting.

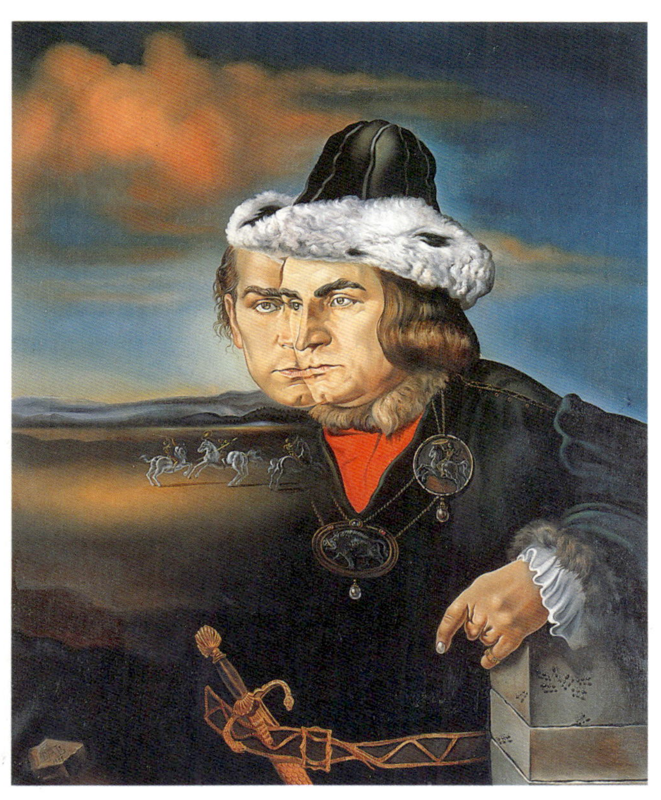

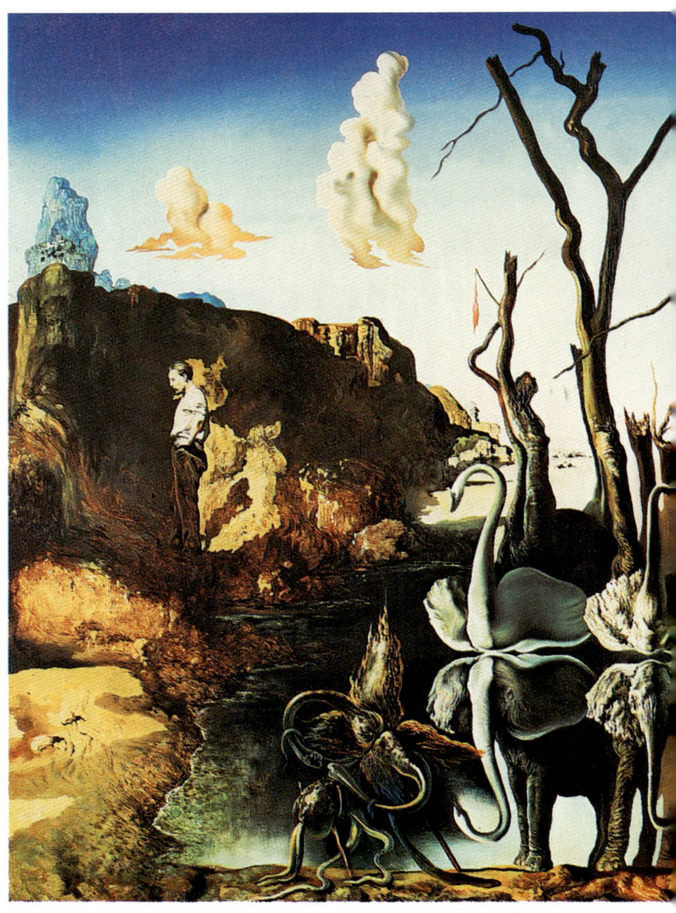

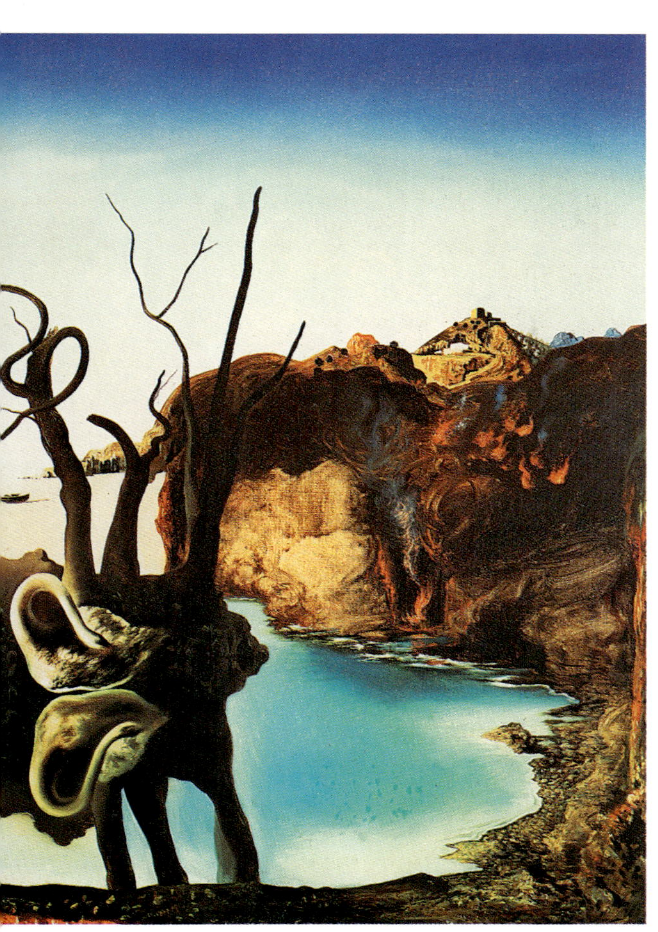

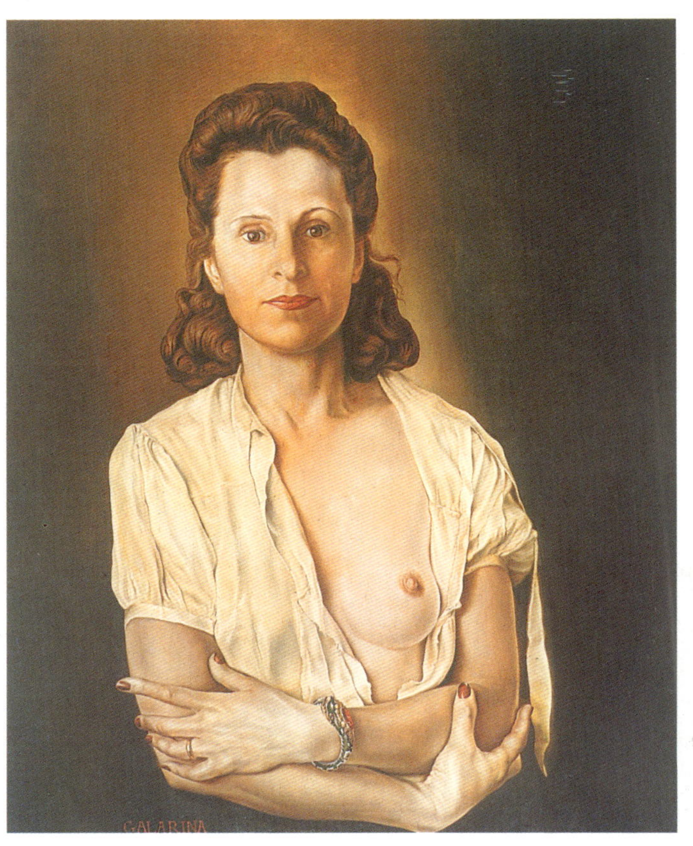
GALARINA

GALARINA, 1944-45. *left*

An intricately observed portrait of the painter's wife. Dali uses Renaissance conventions of light, poise and shadow but cannot resist subverting these, by having Gala display her left breast provocatively.

METAMORPHOSIS OF NARCISSUS, 1937. *overleaf*

Dali's interpretation of the ancient myth comments on the cycle of evolution, from Narcissus' fascination with his own reflection to the appearance of the flower named after him. The childhood experience of seeing one's reflection for the first time is evoked.

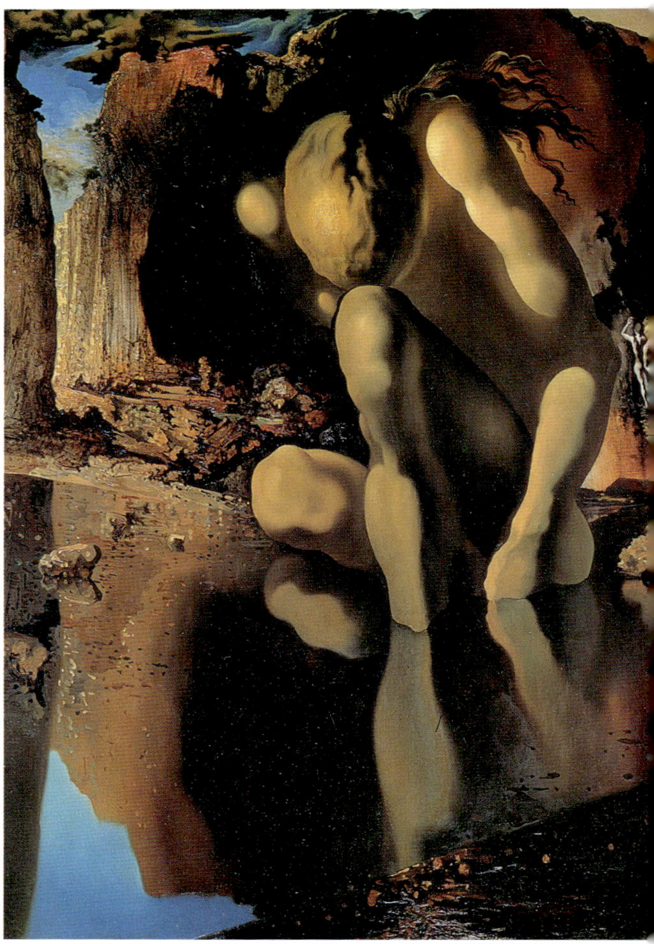

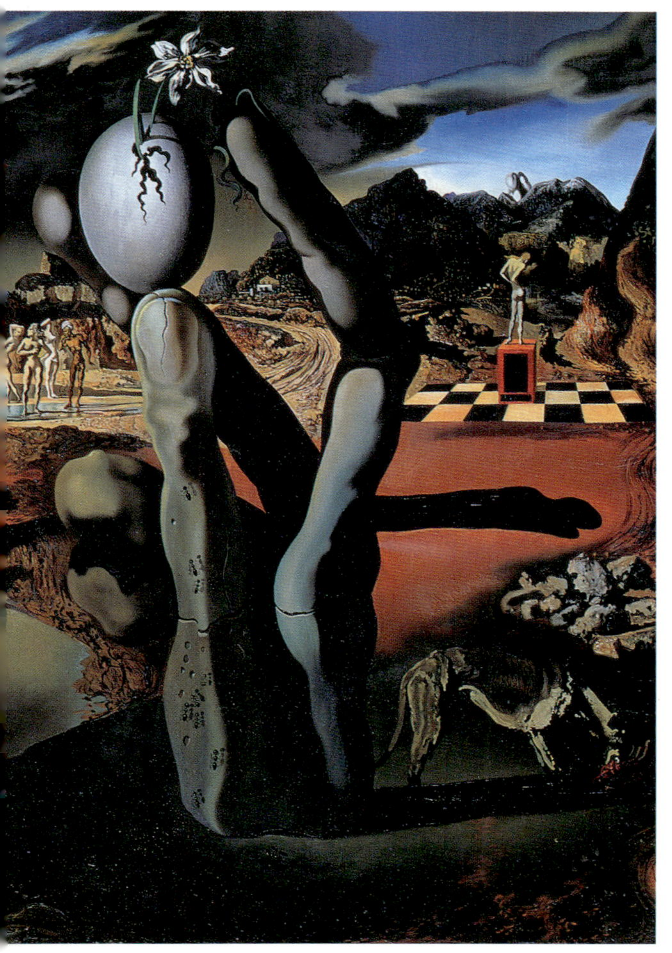

Soft Construction with Boiled Beans: Premonition of Civil War, 1936. *right*

Dali's comment on the outbreak of the Spanish Civil War shows a grotesquely formed human figure in the act of mutilating itself. The agonised, strained expression foretells the destruction that the war was to generate.

Sublime Moment, 1938. *overleaf*

The shattered telephone hanging on a branch alludes to Dali's fear of the consequences of the Munich agreement between Hitler and Neville Chamberlain. The slow drip onto the plate of eggs may indicate the swift passage of time in the last months of peace, and the dismal landscape anticipates the destruction of impending world war.

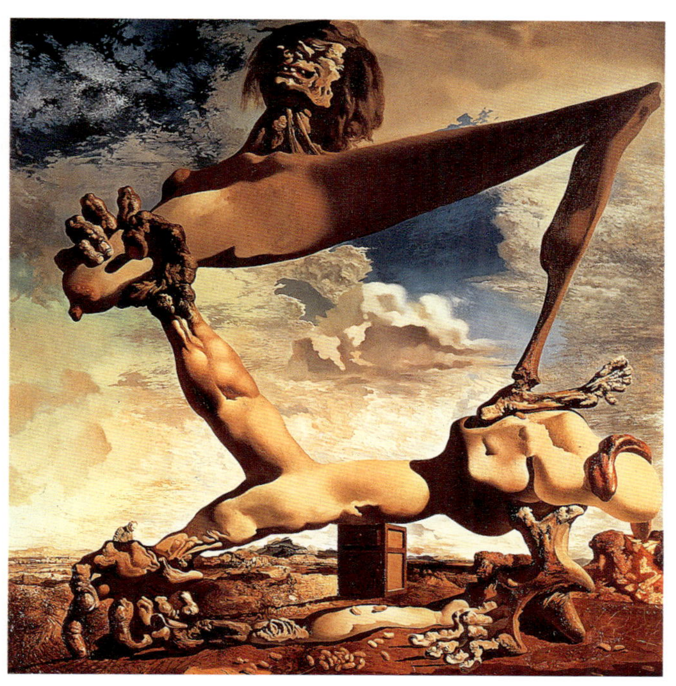

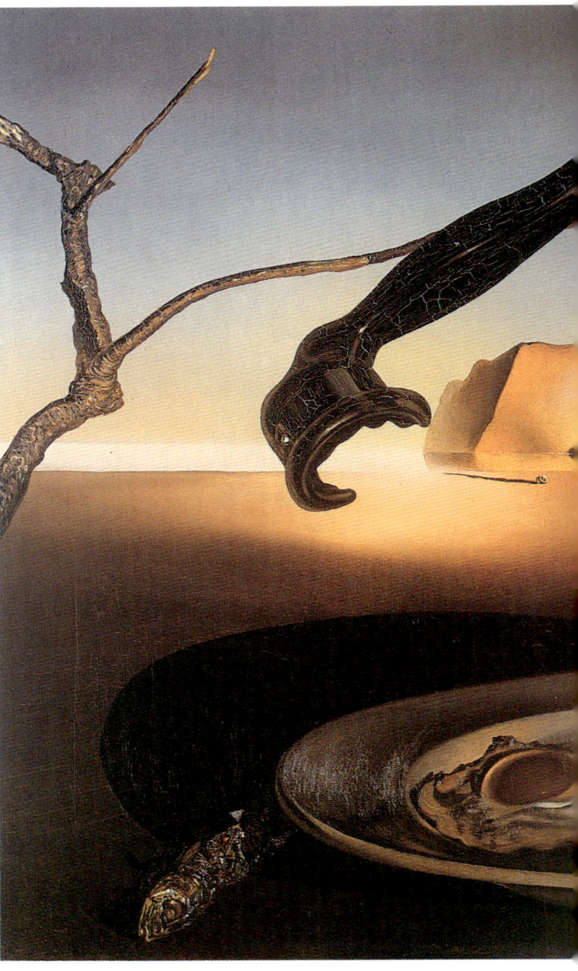

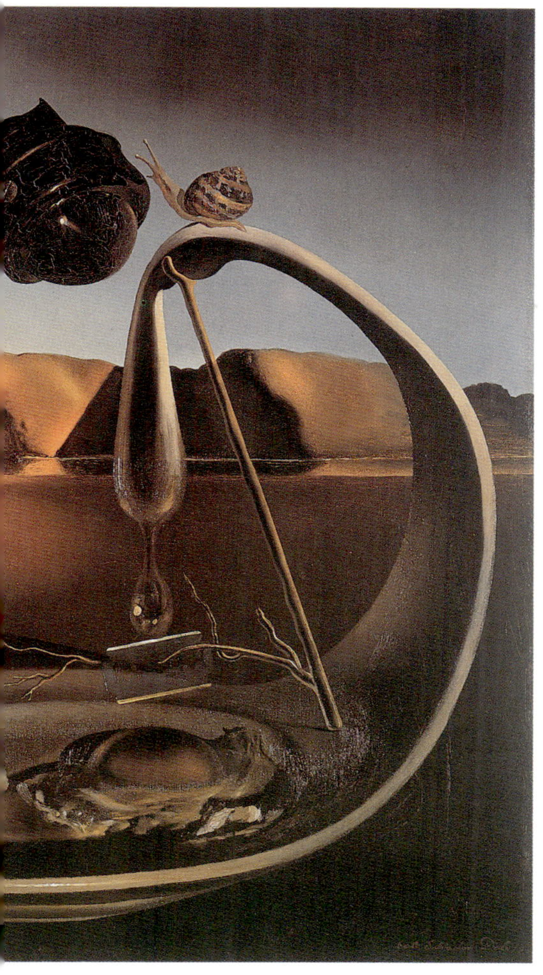

The Bleeding Roses, 1930. *right*

A disturbing image of sexual anxiety and guilt. Dali makes use of the full range of the rose's iconic signification of woman; woman as source of nature, as example of beauty, as driven by atavistic urges to bear children, and the pain involved in the processes of menstruation, reproduction and childbirth.

The Persistence of Memory, 1931. *overleaf*

In this image of decay, flies cover the surface of the watch at bottom left, whilst the literal melting away of the hours point to individual mortality. The seal-like shape in the centre of the work is actually a self-portrait, depicted as withering away in sleep. Dali's miniaturist technique is seen in the careful attention paid to the rock formation, and the mirrored surface of the sea.

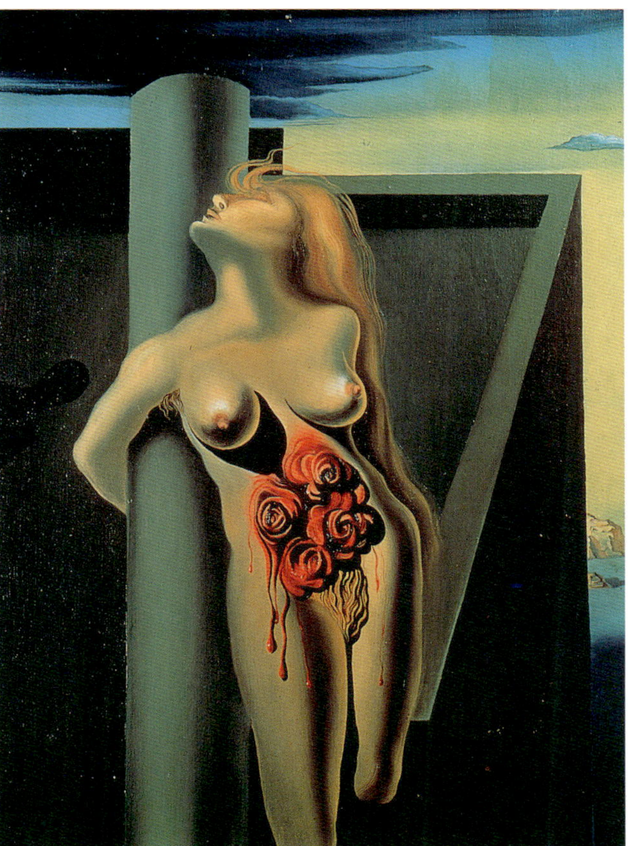

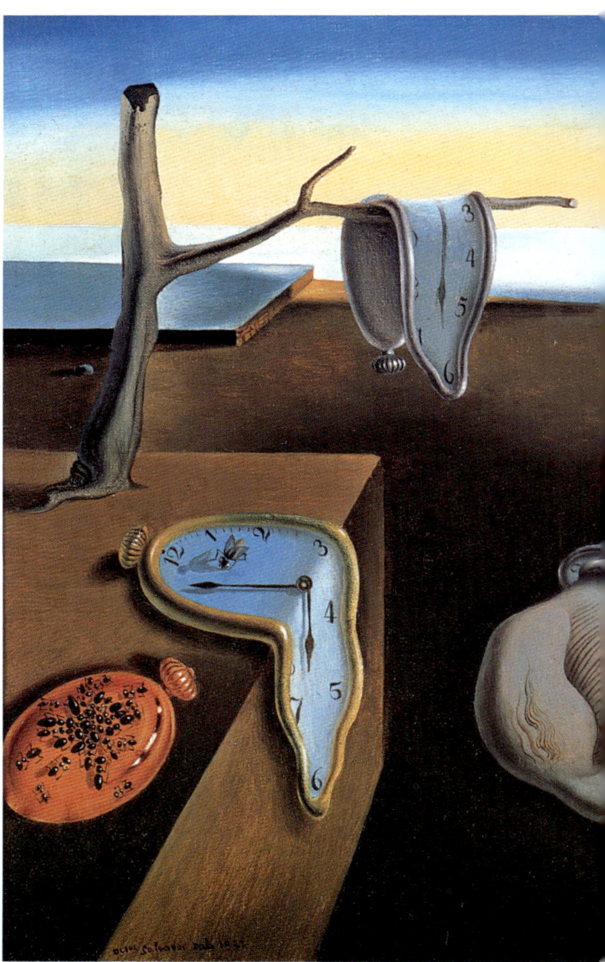

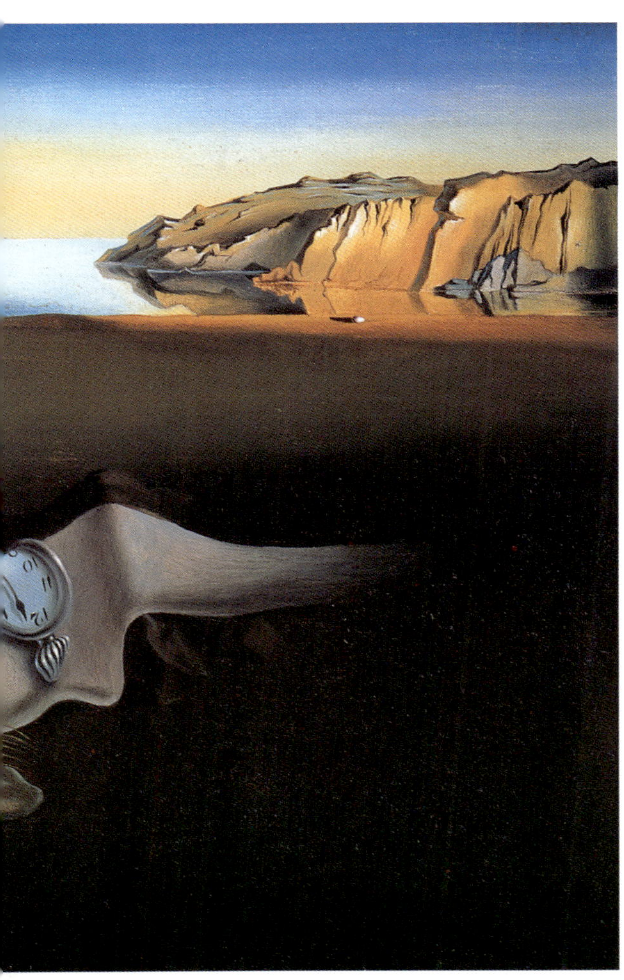

Portrait of a Passionate Lady, 1945. *right*

The gracefully shaped woman's hands and the red varnished nails are arresting symbols of sexual allure. Yet simultaneously, an air of menace is created, by their huge dimension and the way in which they are poised over the idyllic figures beneath. The recurrence of the melting watch motif suggests the transience of relationships between man and woman.

Sleep, 1933. *overleaf*

Sleep was central to Surrealist practice for the dream imagery that they relied upon. The crutches propping up the figure are a Dalinean symbol for unconsciousness: when the individual awakes, the crutches fall away, leading to the sensation of 'falling' which Dali linked to the experience of being born.

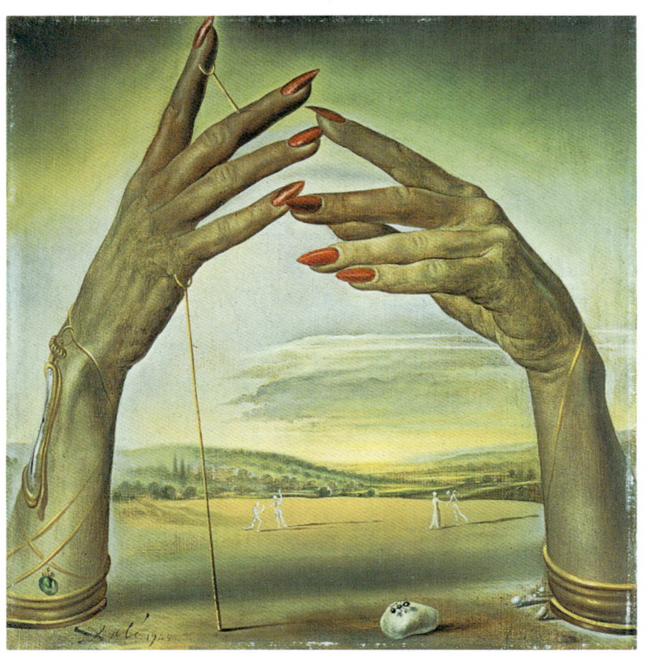

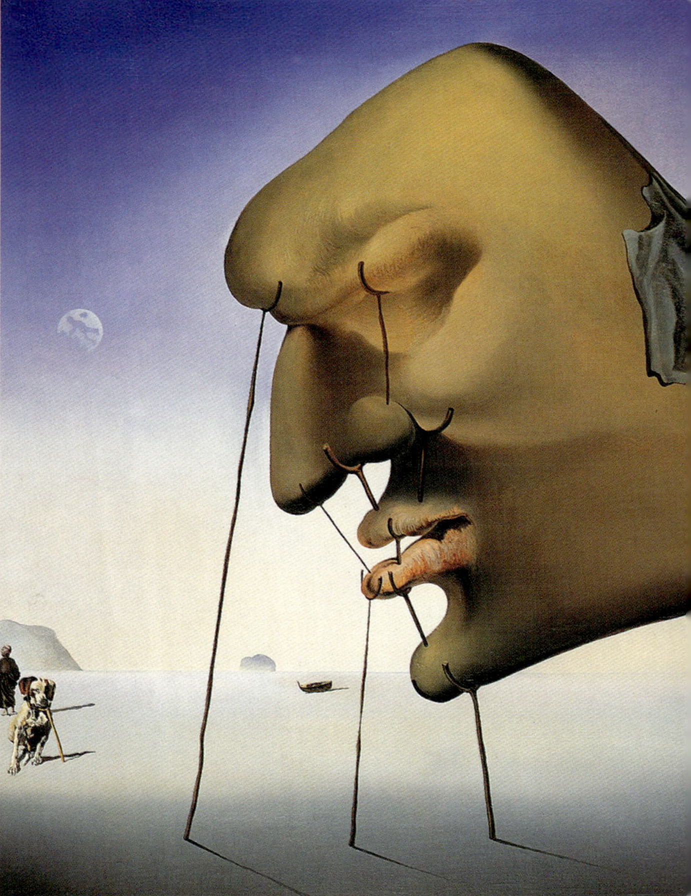

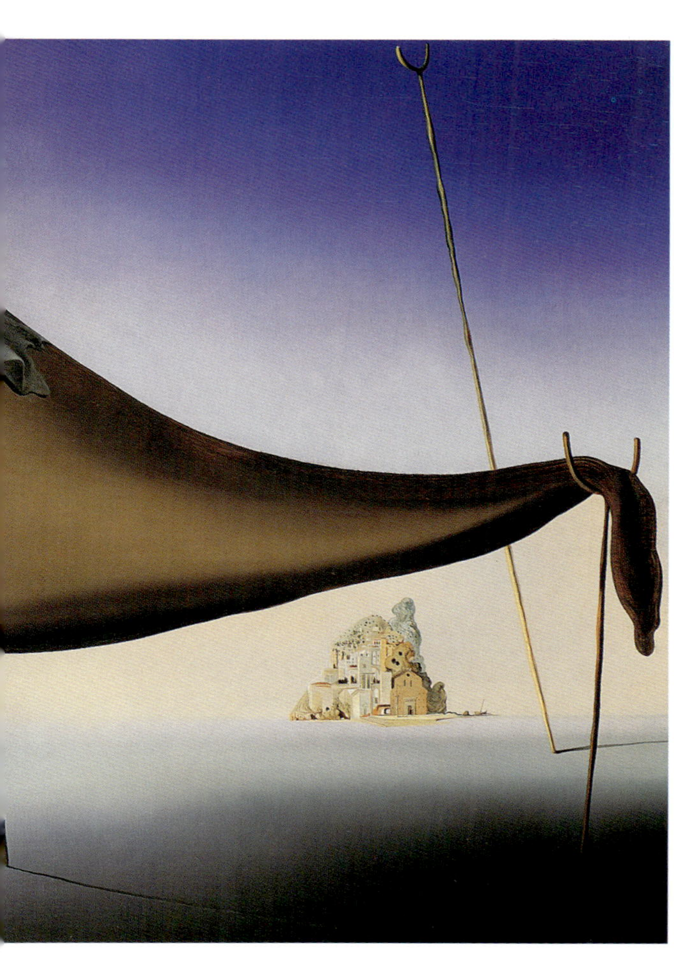

Atavistic Traces after the Rain, 1934. *right*

Dali juxtaposes what seems to be a giant goat's skull with rock outcrops and a distant modern town. The eerie quality of the painting and the detail of the landscape points to Dali's interest in the Swiss mythical landscape painter Arnold Bocklin.

Nude Woman in the Desert, 1948. *overleaf*

The double image method is again employed to suggest the form of a woman embedded in the outline of desert rock. The menacing spikes of the fantastic cloud forms and the presence of predatory animals suggests that this is a hallucinogenic, erotic reverie.

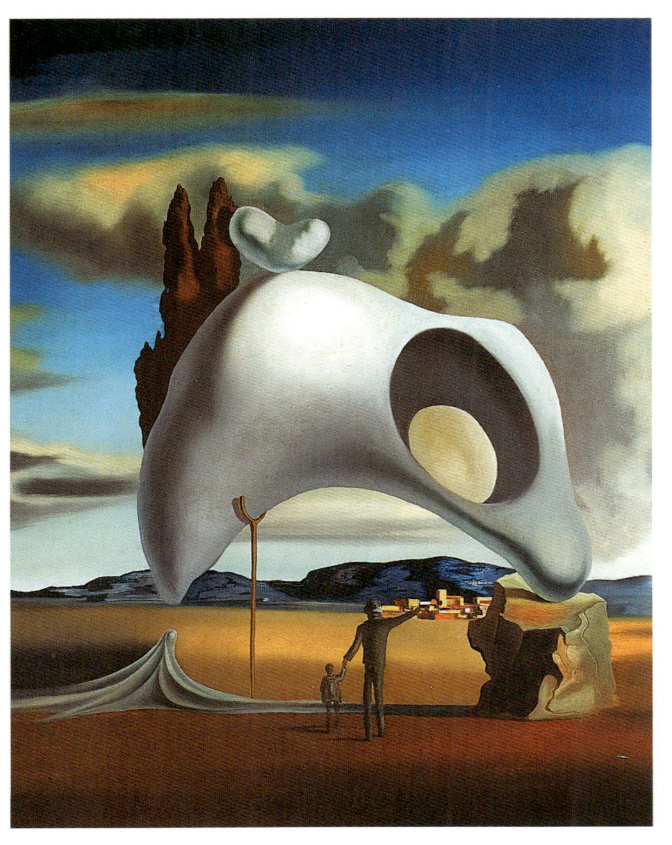

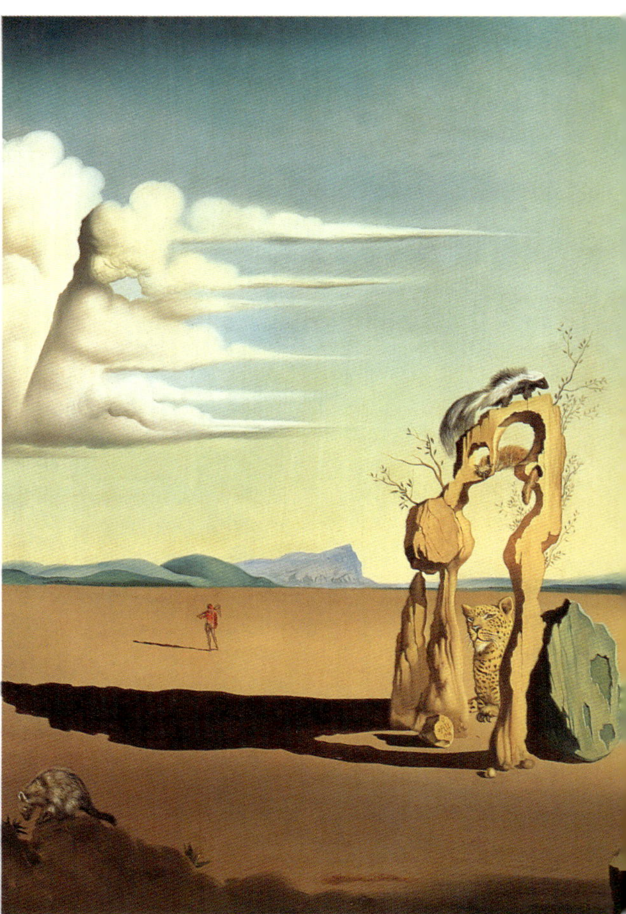

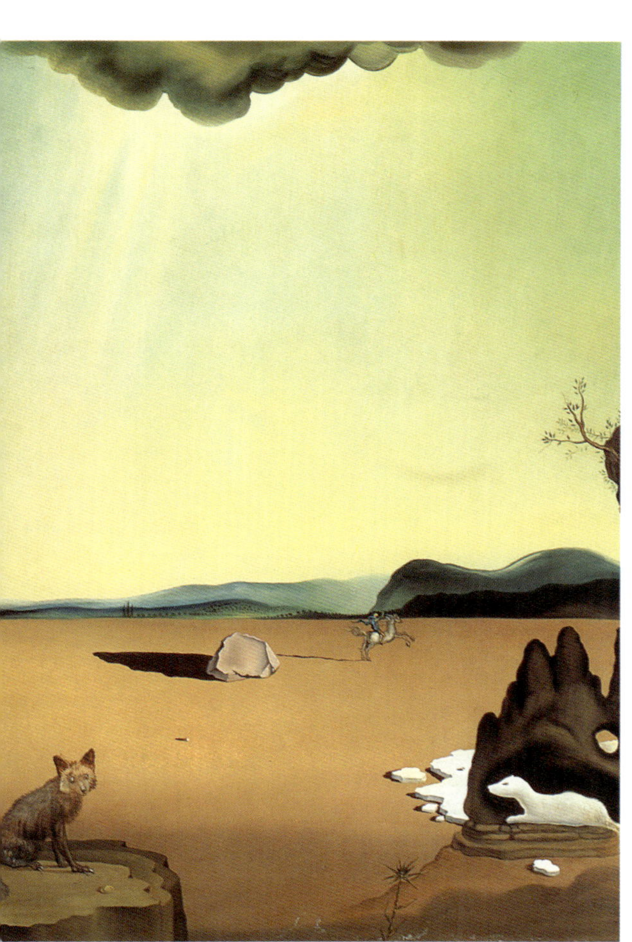

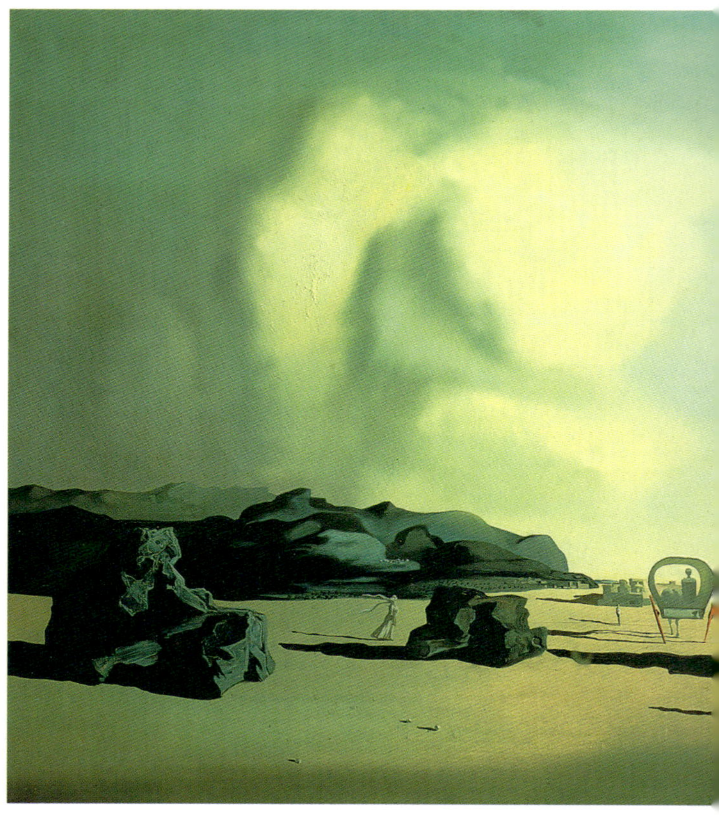

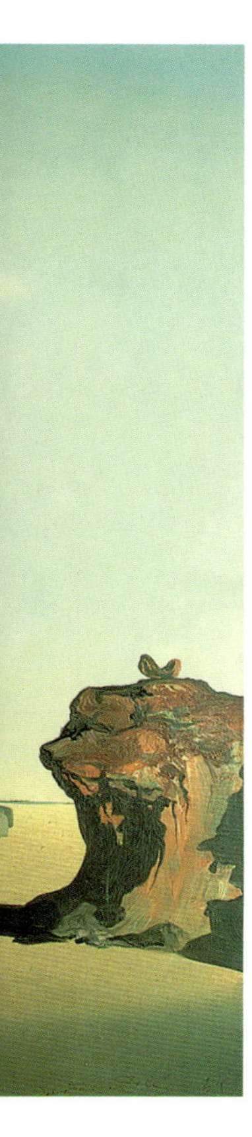

Moment of Transition, 1934.
left Dali's tensile landscape is articulated by means of a familiarly visceral colour orange-red, sand, blue and brown. The chariot image was to recur in later paintings, and other notable Dalinean props are the woman in isolation and menacing rock outcrops throwing off distorted shadows.

Parade de Cavaliers, 1942.
overleaf A range of rearing skeletal horses, observing strict perspectival conventions, mark a grim guard of honour. The rearing horse to the left of the painting seems to be a quote from the Battle of San Romano, by Uccello.

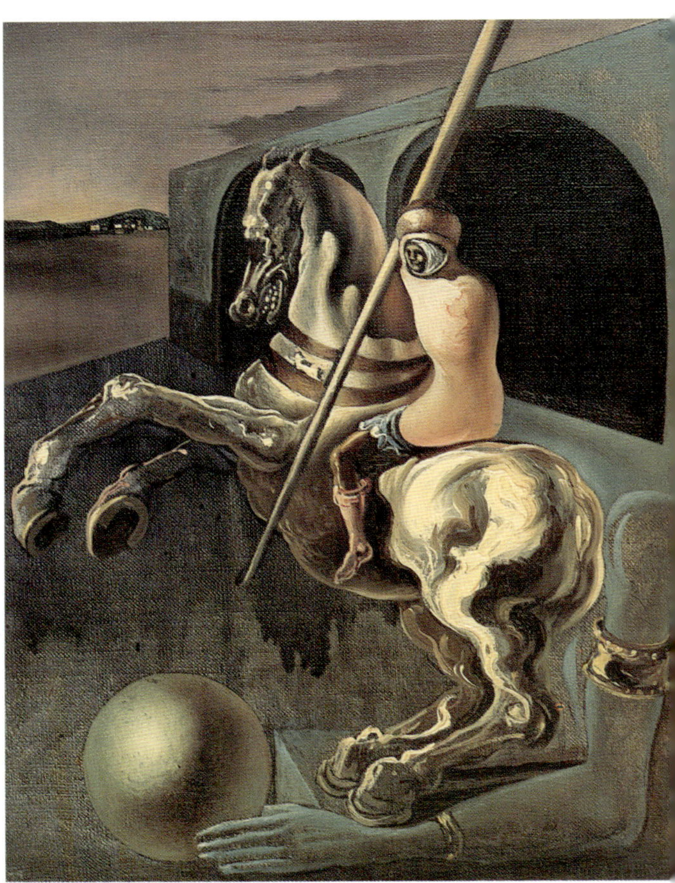

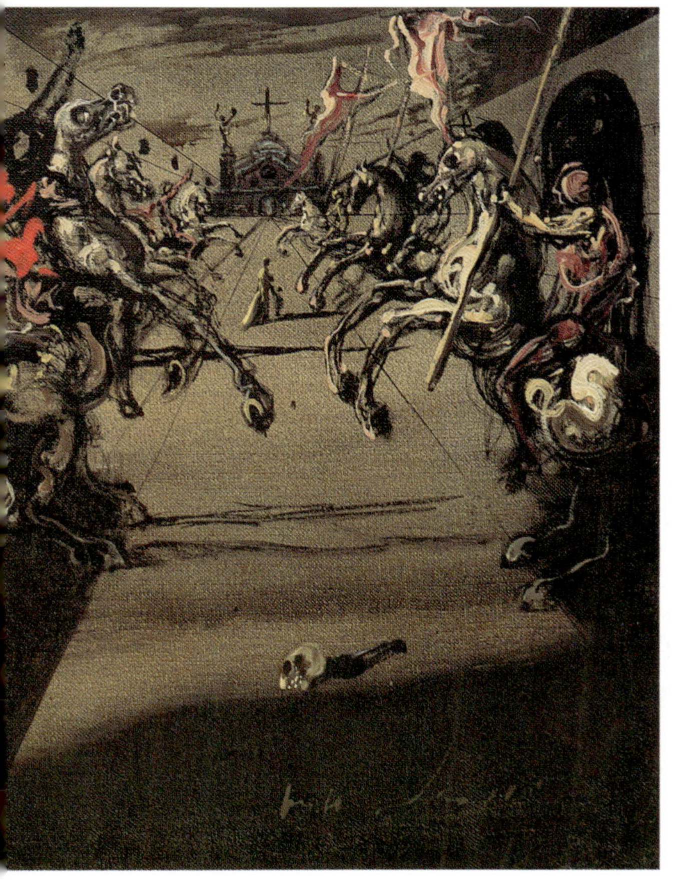

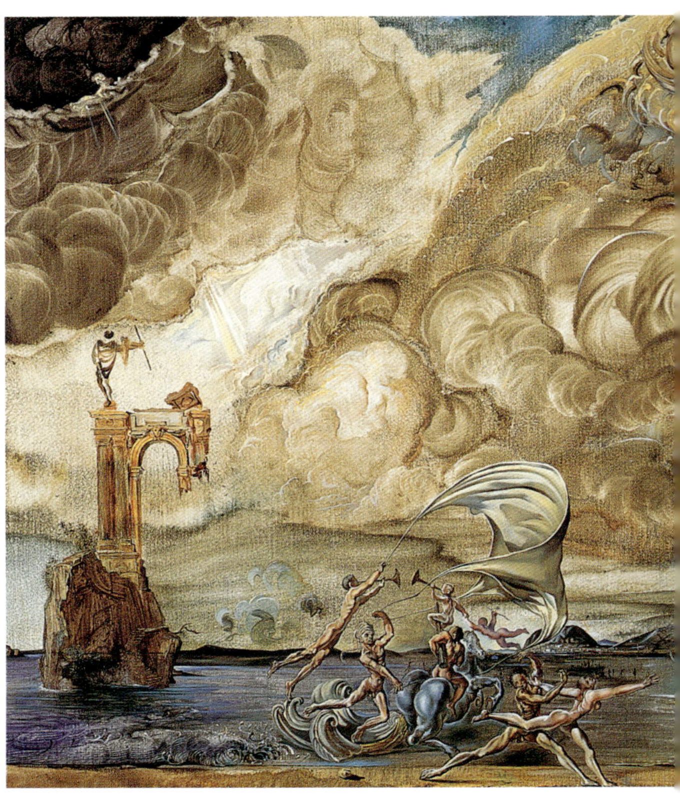

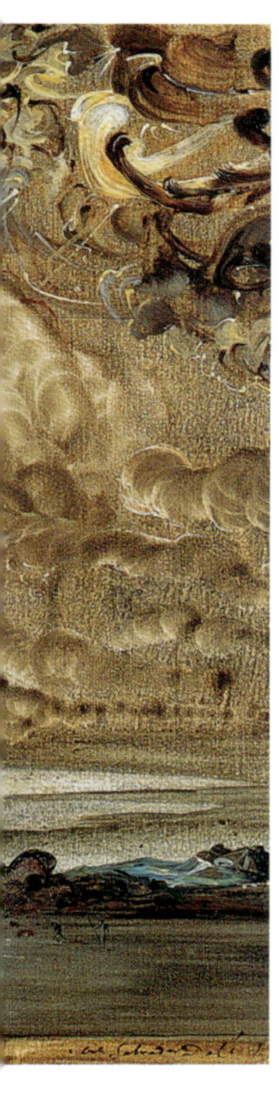

Triumph of the Cyclone, 1943-48. *left*

Classical and Renaissance precedents are evoked in three clear ways; the broken Roman arch, the foregrounded battle scene, and the hint of celestial figures at top right. Perhaps the painting represents a fear that twentieth century progress distanced the individual from the achievements of bygone epochs.

FURTHER READING

Salvador Dali, *Dawn Ades*, Thames & Hudson, London, 1982.

Salvador Dali, Tate Gallery, London, exhibition catalogue, 1980.

Dada and Surrealism Reviewed, Haywood Gallery Catalogue, 1978.

Salvador Dali, James Thrall Soby, New York City, 1946.

Dali, M. Gerard, New York City, 1968.

Dali, J. G.Ballard, London 1974.

Surrealism and Painting, Andre Breton, translated by S.W. Taylor, London, 1978.

PICTORIAL ACKNOWLEDGMENTS

Paranoiac-Critical Solitude, Suburb of the Paranoiac, Image Mediumnique-Parnoique, Sleep, courtesy of **Christes Images.** Lawrence Olivier, Nude Woman in the Desert, courtesy of **Sotheby's Picture Library.** Metamorphosis of Narcissus, courtesy of **Tate Gallery Publishing Limited.** All other pictures courtesy of **AKG London.**

OTHER TITLES IN THIS SERIES

Paul Gauguin

Caspar David Friedrich

Celtic Art

Hokusai

Allen Jones

Pre-Raphaelites

Illuminated Manuscripts

First published in Great Britain in 1997 by **Brockhampton Press**
20 Bloomsbury Street, London WC1B 3QA
a member of the **Hodder Headline Group**

ISBN 1 86019 484 2
A copy of the CIP data is available from the British Library upon request.

Designed and produced for **Brockhampton Press**
by Keith Pointing Design Consultancy.
Text written by Jonathan Blackwood M.A.

Printed and Bound in Italy by L.E.G.O. Spa.